W9-AWS-820

8 Critical Things Your

Auto Accident Attorney Won't Tell You

Why and How to Prepare so You Get the Best When You Need it Most

By Paul A. Samakow, Attorney At Law
Licensed in Maryland and Virginia
Law Practice Limited to Injury & Accident Cases

This book proudly printed in the United States.

13 digit ISBN: 978-0-615-30795-4 - $19.95 retail
10 digit ISBN: 0-615-30795-7 - $19.95 retail

The Law Offices of Paul A. Samakow, P.C.
8230 Old Courthouse Road #430
Tyson's Corner, VA 22182
www.samakowlaw.com

Table of Contents

INTRODUCTION

I wrote this book 5 years ago to educate you. I am now updating and adding important information. I have been practicing law since 1980, almost 35 years now, and I have seen too many clients come to me with complaints about lawyers, hoping I was "better" and asking if I would take their case. The two top complaints about lawyers are that they don't communicate with their clients and that they don't tell them what is going on. What I will tell you, and what I'd tell any lawyer, is that a lawyer must be 100%, totally honest with his clients, and he must tell them everything, before they need to know, so that they can make intelligent and informed decisions.

My time, every working day, is devoted to helping injury and auto accident victims. I am committed to fighting the big insurance companies who see people as numbers, and to delivering stellar and honest legal services. The problem is that sometimes the legal system gets in the way of delivering that help. And sometimes, it is the lawyers who get in the way.

In today's environment of skepticism and tough economic times, there are hundreds of facts and even more interpretations of those facts that can affect the many aspects of a client's legal case. And even if we forget the legal case, there are many considerations that can directly affect the client and the quality of his or her life that direct the course of action that needs to be followed correctly. Events and actions which should be routine, expected and simple, such as getting your car fixed and getting medical care, are sometimes fraught with problems, mostly because of the insurance industry and its attitude toward paying you, and sometimes because of victims' lack of knowledge on what can be described as the "what, when and how" of doing things.

In this book I describe what I have seen over the many years of my practice and I hope to help you by sharing some of my knowledge and observations, so that if and when you get into a car accident, you will have the best chance to minimize the real life problems and to maximize the results of your legal case. Part of that chance involves understanding lawyers.

1

FROM THE AUTHOR

Thank you for reading this book. You will get value, and I would sincerely appreciate your comments.

If you have been injured in a car accident, or if someone you care about has been injured, I'll bet you are concerned about what will happen next. There are immediately many problems and emotions that will suddenly appear because of the accident, not to mention the physical pain. You might naturally wonder about how medical bills will be paid, how your car is going to get fixed, what doctor to see, whether you should talk to insurance company people, how you're going to manage financially because you can't work now, and on and on. So, you don't need problems with or because of your lawyer.

My name is Paul Samakow, and I am an attorney. I practice in Maryland and Virginia. I have been an attorney since 1980 and for over the last 29 years I have done nothing but represent people who have been injured. I have NEVER represented an insurance company. I am a plaintiff's lawyer, and I am proud to say that. My personality would never allow me to represent the interests of an insurance company. Insurance claims representative generally care more about the "bottom line" for their employer than the do about victims whom their insured hurt. Conversely, I care about victims and my professional goal in life is to help as many people as I can, because I know that they are not armed with the information or the tools to help themselves.

I am on a crusade against insurance companies. They are not your friends. Their goal is SOLELY to profit. The less money they pay victims, the more they profit. Insurance adjusters may be very nice people, but they are trying to do a good job for their boss and the company they work for, and that means ultimately paying you less, or not at all. Adjusters don't get raises or promotions by paying you MORE money.

Today, and particularly in tough economic times, people who are injured need straight answers to their questions. I am upset that when accident victims are most stressed, in the aftermath of the accident, and in the days and weeks that follow, insurers try to take advantage. Insurance companies hire people to listen to police radio frequencies and when they hear an accident has occurred they send someone to the victim's house, or call them, and offer them some money to pay for medical bills if they later find they are hurt. Insurance companies employ trained professionals, adjusters, investigation people, and lawyers, all with the goal of figuring out ways to pay you less or not at all. They take pictures of your car from angles to make it look like there's not much damage, and then the adjusters tell you that they can't understand how you could have any injury, given that there wasn't much damage to your car.

If you have been in an automobile accident, I'd love to be your lawyer, however I wrote this book and I'm giving it away for free because I want you to have the information I'm providing here. Whether you hire me, or another lawyer, or no one at all, you are better off with this information, so if you're reading this book, and I never meet you, I know I've done a good thing.

There are some things you absolutely must know. Obtaining compensation from insurance companies is really hard, and it is fraught with obstacles you may never know about and will never realize hit you. Because things are so hard and so complicated, many people don't even try to fight for their rights. Many more mistakenly believe that getting a lawyer will delay things, that the lawyer's fee will mean they get less, or that the lawyer won't be honest with them.

You absolutely must know the following:

1. Even if you are reasonable and honest with the insurance company, they will not give you a fair settlement.

2. You do not have to talk to insurance adjusters, and you do not have to let them record anything. If they tell you the opposite, that you must allow a recorded statement in order to get benefits or for them to pay your claim, they are lying.

3. The insurance company for the person at fault does not have to pay your medical bills as you incur them.

4. It is not true that "somebody" has to pay even though it wasn't your fault.

5. Going to court does not assure you will win.

6. Maryland and Virginia juries are not sympathetic and they will not give you the money you think you should get.

There are some really bad and costly consequences you could encounter after an accident and during the claims process.

1. The insurance company will act slowly (this is the rule, rather than the exception).

2. The person at fault may not report the accident, causing further delay.

3. The person at fault may not have any insurance, or not enough insurance, meaning you will have to use the Uninsured Motorist or the Under-insured Motorist provisions of your insurance policy.

4. Your car could cost more to repair than it is worth.

5. If your car was destroyed (that is called a total loss) and you owe more money than it is worth, you could end up with no car and owing money on it. "GAP" (Guaranteed Auto Protection) Insurance by the way, is an answer for this problem. Call your insurance agent and ask for this when you buy a new car.

I believe that in most cases you need a lawyer. This book is designed to help you understand how lawyers work. Before I tell you what lawyers won't tell you, consider these things:

1. Most people don't know a lawyer, and they believe it will cost too much to hire a lawyer. In auto accident injury cases, it will not cost you anything "up front." Lawyers uniformly work on contingent fees, meaning they take a percentage of the recovery, usually one-third of the settlement.

2. Most people aren't sure if they can trust a lawyer, so they don't want to hire one. That is why I'm writing this book. Use it if you get into an accident when you hire your lawyer!

3. Most people believe when an insurance adjuster tells them that they will end up with less money if they hire an attorney. So in order to avoid legal fees, they try to represent themselves. Bad idea. A study done every year by a group called the Insurance Institute finds, every year, that people with lawyers end up with more money, even after the lawyer's fee is deducted, than they would have gotten without the lawyer. Why do you think insurance companies work so hard to convince you to settle early? Because they know that once you get a lawyer, they're going to pay more.

4. Many people who are victims, who are now physically and psychologically stressed, who are financially pressed, and who are also depressed, don't want to be bothered by the hassle of making a claim and they do nothing, thus jeopardizing their rights to full compensation. Certain things cannot be erased, like giving a recorded statement to the adjuster where you've said things that hurt your case. Also, delaying getting a lawyer can result in evidence or witnesses being lost.

I wrote this book with one question in mind: "If my loved one was in an accident, and I couldn't help them, what would I want him or her to know?" So I will tell you what I'd tell my loved one, and what most auto accident lawyers will not tell you, so you will be fully informed.

Unfortunately, there are many lawyers that will pressure you. They spend a lot of money to get you to become their client. They advertise "CASH" or "GET ALL YOU DESERVE" on TV or in the Yellow Pages, and then they have you come in for a free consultation. Then passively, or sometimes even aggressively, they pressure you to sign a contract making them your lawyer. Then, once you hire them, you never see them or hear from them until they tell you to settle your case for an amount of money you never were consulted about or agreed to. I despise that type of behavior. Picking an attorney is very important. An accident or an injury can be one of the most horrible and stressful events that life can offer. I know because I've represented thousands and thousands of clients and I've seen what happens, particularly if someone has been seriously injured, permanently impaired, or killed.

With constant changes in injury laws and with the continuing aggressiveness of insurance companies, I'm nervous that you may not get the help you need. The last thing you need is to be taken advantage of by an insurance company, or by your own lawyer.

Some cases don't require an attorney. I don't take cases if the only problem after the accident is damage to your car. My first response to people calling me in these cases is "Thank God you were not hurt." Even if you have a minor injury, you may not need a lawyer. If you went to the hospital just to get yourself checked out, or some time has gone by and you went to your doctor once or twice, and nothing is wrong, again, great! Whether you were at fault, or not, your auto insurance policy may have provisions that allow you to force them to fix your car, to provide a rental car, to pay for towing, and to pay medical bills up to some predetermined amount. You don't need a lawyer to accomplish these types of things.

I wrote this book because I want you to know as much as possible about getting money from insurance companies. I know most of the tricks we lawyers use and I know why. This book is an honest and an educational guide to help you navigate, with the assistance of a good lawyer, this very upsetting and trying time in your life. By telling you what most lawyers won't tell you, I'm helping you get more money.

If you have been injured, I hope you recover quickly. Keep reading and if you learn even one thing that helps guide you through this process, I've succeeded.

I disclose EVERYTHING to my clients and to potential clients. Call me with ANY question. 703-761-4343 or 301-949-1515.

Chapter 1

What to Expect from the Insurance Company after an Accident

Your attorney will tell you what I am now going to discuss. I included this information now, and here, because it is important for anybody who is a victim of an automobile accident to know. Beginning with the next chapter, I'll tell you what most auto accident lawyers will not tell you.

I highly recommend always talking to an attorney before you talk to any insurance company representative or adjuster. Speaking to an attorney first can give you information, which will be useful both immediately and long term as you deal with the numerous issues surrounding being involved in a car accident. Sometimes however, before you talk to the attorney, the adjuster calls you, or the adjuster may even, outrageously, come to your house without calling you at all.

First, remember the basic tenet. Insurance companies are not your friends. Their only goal is to save money, not give it to you, whether or not you are entitled. They will stall, delay and often tell you things that have various levels of truth, and often fail to tell you things you should know. So, you might hear from an insurance claims adjuster, seemingly, almost immediately. You should make sure you know which insurance company is calling you. Sometimes adjusters actually appear at your door without notice. It will either be your company, or the at fault party's company. It is important to know because what you say to them can make a difference later. Most people who are injured, amazingly, are often more concerned about their car, and getting it repaired. First calls from the other person's insurance company typically have the goal of "settling" your injury claim with you right away. Don't!!!! Some injuries do not say hello to you until after the adrenaline rush from the accident has dissipated. The insurer "early settlement" tactics include offering you a small amount of money for your suffering, such as $500.00 to $1000.00, and then promising you they'll pay for your medical bills up to $1,000.00 or $2,000.00 if you need care over the next six months. The figures could be higher or lower, but the point is clear, they are trying to get out fast and cheap, before the full extent of the damages are known.

Fault is the first thing the other person's insurer wants to establish. Often, the adjuster will tell you they can't help you until they talk to their insured to get their side of the story. They will want you to tell them what happened and they will want to record the telephone call with you. Unless the accident was an absolutely clear, rear-end when you were stopped type of case, do not tell them how the accident happened. The benefit of you talking to them is much less than the potential damage you can cause by talking to them. While trying to be "honest" you might inadvertently say things that can hurt your case later. Trust that these adjusters are trained and will ask you things in a way to elicit these harmful statements from you.

There are two things of concern initially. You are number one, and issues concerning your now damaged car are number two. If you are engaged in conversation with the other party's insurance, be careful!

If you do decide to talk to the other party's adjuster, or you are pressed to talk to them because they won't agree to take care of your car unless you do, limit the discussion to only how the accident happened AND do not allow them to record the conversation. Under no circumstances should you discuss whether you were injured or what injuries you suffered. Your medical records will contain that information. The adjuster, upon your refusal to discuss injuries may say something like "Well, are you injured?" You should repeat that you are not going to discuss injuries and state that you will not answer that question. The adjuster may tell you they want to send a medical release or authorization for you to sign, so they can make it easy for you and that they will get your medical records. Again, NO WAY! These authorizations often are very broad and allow the adjuster to obtain more information than they need, or that you'd want them to have. Further, it is wise to review your records for mistakes before the other party's insurer gets them, as those mistakes could be costly to your claim.

The other party's insurer is responsible for repairing your car, or for paying you the value of your car if it is declared a "total loss." They are also responsible to pay for "replacement transportation," meaning a rental car. They are not required to provide a rental car of the quality of your vehicle. So if you have a sports car or a luxury car, all you are legally entitled to is a run of the mill small or medium sized sedan.

Now, concerning your insurance company's contact. You should report the accident, and you are required to cooperate with your company in the investigation of the claim. So, it is fine to talk to them about how the accident happened, but again, I would caution discussing your injury situation at this first contact. Your company, if you have the coverage on your policy, will undertake to repair your car and provide you a rental car. This is fine, and you should not be concerned about your rates going up. Your rates cannot and will not go up because you use your benefits. Your health insurance premiums don't go up because you use your health benefits. Also, your insurer will get their money back from the other person's insurer later on.

So to conclude, insurance companies are not your friends. For car damage claims only, most of the time you do not need a lawyer. If you were injured, contact an attorney before talking to the adjusters. Nothing is going to be lost by delays of a day or two so that you can first talk to a lawyer. Then, if you decide to hire a lawyer, he or she will do all of the talking for you, and your job is to get better. That way, you won't have to be concerned about what you might say that can hurt your case.

DO NOT TALK TO INSURANCE REPRESENTATIVES FIRST. CALL ME. I WILL GIVE YOU A 100% FREE CONSULTATION.

703-761-4343 or 301-949-1515 or paul@samakowlaw.com

I will provide you with an absolutely FREE review of your Insurance Policy. You can even send it to me by FAX or email and I will reply. Most people do not want to take the time for something like this. Therefore, I will make it easy for you. My fax # is 703-761-4349. My email is paul@samakowlaw.com. All I need is your "Declarations Page" to see what you have and what you do not.

Chapter 2

The Eight Critical Things Your Auto Accident Attorney Won't Tell You

Critical Thing #1 You May Not Be Told:
How Your Case Will Be Managed

Practicing law is, in part, a business. Most business owners will not disclose to their customers all the intricacies of how the business is run. Lawyers, in this business mode, are like business owners. They will not always tell their clients how everything works, because first, how a business runs is often proprietary, and second, the day to day and long term management decisions are not things lawyers want to discuss with clients. By analogy, consumers don't routinely inquire about procedures in and decisions about the running of a restaurant. They go there and expect good food and beverage, courteous service, and a fair price. How the menu was printed, the design of the rooms, the accounting system used, the salaries of the waiters, and more business decisions are not the things made known to the customers. Further, restaurant owners are not going to invite you into the kitchen and show you how their chefs prepare the meals or what ingredients they use.

Individuals who have been involved in an auto accident, from my experience, want a lawyer to tell them their rights. People want help in securing those rights, meaning often helping them with car repair, keeping the insurance companies away from them, getting needed medical care paid for, and getting money lost from not being able to work at their job reimbursed. It also means getting an additional amount of compensation to pay them for their pain, suffering, inconvenience and aggravation. In more serious cases, lawyers are sought out to help assure that there is money to fully compensate problems that may be permanent or cause future financial hardships.

Before I discuss then what most lawyers won't tell their clients, I must tell you that lawyers should do what they were trained to do, and what they are best at, and that is legal work. Lawyers should be the ones making the decisions, strategizing and being the overall "coach" of your case. It's okay that the coach doesn't actually do all of the work. It is like the football coach who sends in plays for the team to carry out. Most lawyers will not tell their clients that paralegals, clerks and other administrative staff will routinely handle most of the matters relating to the case.

Clients may not initially feel comfortable being told a paralegal is going to do most of the administrative work on their case. A client may feel they are hiring a lawyer and they may believe that the lawyer will be doing all of the work. In fairness, these expectations are not reasonable, nor consistent with an efficient running of a law practice. Some lawyers will "skip" this discussion. I don't believe this discussion should be skipped and I make sure potential clients know this and approve of it before they hire me. If they don't get it, or don't approve, they are free to go to another lawyer.

So staff will be in charge of getting the police report, collecting medical and billing information from medical providers, dealing with property damage matters, getting documentation about wage loss, and administratively handling insurance company contacts. Staff will routinely deal with insurance benefits, such as a client's health insurance and their automobile insurance Medical Payments or Personal Injury Protection (PIP) benefits.

I believe when you hire an attorney, the attorney is the one who should negotiate your injury settlement with the other person's insurance companies, no matter how big or how small the case. Some lawyers who do not agree with me will probably never tell you that they have their non-lawyer staff do that for them in many small or routine cases.

My opinion about the lawyer being the negotiator is actually the same as stated in the Ethics Rules in most states. The lawyers who use non-lawyer staff to negotiate justify that practice and point to the Ethics Rules that state that a non-lawyer may do the negotiating if that non-lawyer is under the supervision of the lawyer and that the negotiations are at the direction of the lawyer. So, technically, the Ethics Rules allow non- lawyer staff to be the communicators for the lawyer who is supposed to be doing the thinking and strategizing and the "back and forth" during the negotiations.

Make sure you ask your injury lawyer about all of this. Delegation to non-lawyer staff is fine and necessary to the proper running of a law office. Just be clear with your lawyer what you expect.

My staff handles a great deal of the administrative

tasks for my clients' cases. I am the only one who

evaluates and settles cases. I owe that to my clients.

Call me if you want to make sure your case is resolved

by an attorney - me. 703-761-4343 or 301-949-1515.

Critical Thing #2 You May Not Be Told:
Getting Your Car Fixed Can Be
Maddening

Cars seem to be the single most important thing to people after an accident, even if they are injured. I do get it. The car takes us where we want and need to go, and we figure that we'll be okay, but the car.... Oh my... who is going to pay to fix it? What will we do while it's being fixed? Yes, very reasonable concerns, even if not in the right priority.

Your attorney, at the initial meeting, will probably assure you that everything with you car will be taken care of, and not to worry. The attorney, even if not for the most altruistic reason, has the priorities properly appreciated. You are more important than your car.

Thus the car issues are usually not fully discussed during the initial meeting. Attorneys know the following things, and they are sometimes reluctant to fully go into all of them, because doing so might discourage the potential client and result in that individual looking for another attorney before deciding who to hire. So the things are these:

1. The other person's insurance company may not immediately agree to fix your car. They are going to want to investigate the claim first and assure that the person they insure was truly at fault. This delay is certainly reason for you to be upset, as you want your car fixed now. Knowing this, the attorney might delay telling you this until a day or two after you've hired him. In fairness to attorneys, however, this is not always the case. Often the insurers will yank you around, often causing you and others like you to get an attorney, and then after the first call from your

attorney, the insurers suddenly magically agree to start repairing your car. But, sometimes, not. So no absolute answer from the attorney can be provided, and the assurances given by the attorney are usually correct. In cases where the insurer takes more than a few days to decide I typically tell my clients to have their insurance company handle it, or to make arrangements to have it fixed themselves if they don't have insurance.

2. Getting a rental car typically is easy, but if you don't have a credit card, or you are under the age of 25, it could be a bit of a problem. Your attorney may not initially tell you these things, first and foremost, because the matters involving your injury are clearly more important, and secondly, the concern is that the client, again, may look for another attorney if the attorney can't immediately resolve that type of problem.

3. Your attorney may also not tell you that the rental car isn't going to be the same as the car that was damaged. As I mentioned previously in this book, the law requires that the other party's insurer provide you with replacement transportation, not a replacement of your car.

4. Your attorney may not tell you that you may have a limit on the length of time that you can keep the rental car without being charged. If you delay picking up your car after it is repaired, you might end up paying for some of the rental during that delay. Typically, you have 1 or 2 days at most to get your repaired car. If your car was destroyed, typically, again, you will have a short period of time to turn in your rental car after you've received the funds paying you for your car.

5. Regarding your insurance company fixing your car then, you may or may not have collision coverage on your automobile policy. If you did not bring your policy with you so that the lawyer can confirm your coverage, the best the lawyer can tell you is that you probably have the coverage, and that there might be (probably will be) a deductible you'll have to pay to get your insurance company to fix your car. You will normally get that

deductible money back, after the other person's insurer agrees to accept responsibility.

6. Some lawyers, by the way, don't handle car matters at all, and they will tell you that right up front. They only handle the injury portion of your claim. I feel that if a client comes in and honors me (and gives me the opportunity to make money by representing him), I'm going to handle his car problems.

7. Your car may be a total loss. That means that it will cost more money to repair it than it is worth. Actually, the insurance companies use a percentage rule, typically 80%, so that if the repair cost is 80% or more of the value of the car, they will declare it a total loss. Attorneys cannot possibly know, without your description or photographs that make it very obvious, if your car is going to be declared to be a total loss. What they don't tell you is that the insurance companies have some discretion in making the decision. An insurer often would rather pay a bit more and declare the car a total loss than undertake repairs which can lead to aggravations about the quality of the repairs, undiscovered problems their estimator may have initially missed, etc.

8. Also, regarding your now destroyed car, attorneys are reluctant to tell you initially (in fairness because they don't know and shouldn't be expected to know) that you might end up owing money. This situation is commonly called "being up-side down," and it happens when you owe more money on the car than it is currently worth. The likelihood of this situation presenting is smaller and smaller, and results from how much money you borrowed to buy the car (the less you borrowed the sooner you'll be right side up), and when you bought the car (the longer you have owned the car the more you will have paid on the loan, and the less you'll owe).

9. Last but not least, what your attorney will not necessarily tell you about repairs is that they may not be perfect, and that after-market parts are acceptable in some situations. The reasons for not telling you these things are obvious. Clearly, the other guy caused the accident and your car

should be the same after it's fixed. Reality is that your car is metal, and rubber and plastic, and it will never be exactly the same as before the accident. Your choices here are to accept the slight differences, or file a lawsuit, which is rarely a good choice given the difficulty of establishing the monetary value, or loss, caused by the improper repair. Additionally, the costs associated with the lawsuit may make going forward with that lawsuit financially ridiculous. You could "win" the case, but because of the costs involved, you could end up "losing" financially.

To conclude, my advice is adjust your mindset, remember that your car is metal, plastic and rubber, relax, act reasonably and move on.

I am 100% about honesty. I am not going to file a lawsuit for a client to fight over minor car repair matters or a few hundred dollars. There are strategies we use to get maximum results, but sometimes it simply is not worth the "fight" to try to get things back to exactly the way they were before the accident.

I view your injuries as much more important.

Call me at any time to discuss your situation. 703-761-4343 or 301-949-1515.

Critical Thing #3 You May Not Be Told:
I Don't Know How Much Money You'll Get

How much money am I going to get for my case? What is my case worth? One form or another of this basic question is usually one of the first questions most clients ask, and it is absolutely the most difficult question for a lawyer to answer.

Generally speaking, there are a few common factors that determine the value of any personal injury case. These are:

1. The type of injuries you suffered and their duration.
2. The amount of medical bills you incurred in getting treated for those injuries.
3. The amount of money you lost from your job because you weren't able to work or needed to rest to help you recover, and the money you lost because you had to go to therapy for treatment.
4. Compensation for "pain and suffering".

And, if your injuries are permanent:

1. The predicted cost of medical care in the future.
2. The estimated future lost income you will suffer.
3. Compensation for future pain and suffering.

As an experienced personal injury lawyer, I don't usually give potential clients a dollar amount to answer the value question. The reasons are discussed below. I will tell you, however, that after I have all of the information I need, and after my client has fully recovered from his or her injuries (or they have gotten as good as they're going to get if their injuries are permanent) I send my client a letter clearly stating my opinion about the value of their case. In that letter I ask the client's permission to proceed, before I begin any negotiations with the insurance companies. In that letter I tell them what I think the value of their case is, I tell them my fee (1/3 before suit is filed), I tell them what the balance due is for any of their medical bills which are not yet paid, and I tell them how much they will get, or "pocket" after my fee and the medical bills are paid. I also tell them the amount I intend to "demand" when I contact the insurance company. So, as an example, I might tell the client I think their case has a value of $10,000.00, and that I am going to make a "demand" to the insurance company pay us $25,000.00. This bigger demand amount allows me room to negotiate. But let's go back to the valuation discussion and why attorneys are reluctant to address it early on.

To start, and to be fair, personal injury claims are either "small" or "serious". Lawyers can predict the value of small cases, but typically don't want to, and will not tell clients what their estimates are at the early stages of the small case. Lawyers are reluctant to tell prospective clients the value of a small case, because at the beginning, the lawyer doesn't absolutely know it's a small case, and, the lawyer doesn't want the prospective client to hear a small monetary amount for fear that the impression will be "it's not worth it."

Small cases will typically settle with insurance companies for anywhere from $1,000.00 to $20,000.00, depending upon many factors. These factors include the type of injuries, the amount of medical bills, the amount of wages lost, the jurisdiction where the case would go to court if a settlement could not be reached, the age, race, sex and prior medical condition of the client, as well as the overall impression the client would make as a witness if the case had to go to court. Additional factors can include the amount of damage to the victim's car, whether the victim went to the hospital after the accident, which doctor the victim was treated by, and how long it took to actually go to that doctor after the accident. Small cases usually involve what are called "whiplash" injuries, or in

18

other words, muscle injuries, which are located in the neck or the back, or both. These injuries often respond favorably and resolve completely after a month or two of physical therapy or chiropractic care.

The truth is that in many small cases, and this is more and more true the smaller the case, it may not be worth hiring an attorney. An attorney will generally always be able to get more money, but by comparison, in a fairly small case, a higher settlement amount with the attorney's fee deducted may not be as much as the "net" to the client if the client simply negotiated with the insurance company directly. An example is a $2,100.00 settlement produced by the attorney compared to a $1,500.00 settlement obtained by the client without the attorney's involvement. The $2,100.00 settlement "nets" the client $1,400.00 after the attorney takes the typical 1/3 fee (here, $700.00). That would end up being $100.00 less "in the pocket" of the client compared to the client negotiating themselves and getting a $1,500.00 settlement.

As the value of the injury claim increases, the more an attorney is needed. Non-lawyers cannot seriously threaten an insurance company. If a non-lawyer tries to negotiate their own settlement, and gets a low offer from the insurance adjuster, the most that non-lawyer can do is tell the adjuster that they are going to go get a lawyer. Statistically, most people never get the lawyer, and they end up calling the adjuster back and accepting the low offer. A lawyer, on the other hand, has the ability to threaten the insurance company. The threat is going to court. So again, because of this lack of threatening power, insurers are typically unwilling to make "fair" offers directly to accident victims. They have no incentive to do so. It requires the intervention of an attorney, who can force them into court if a fair amount isn't offered, to produce a fair settlement offer. Then, comparing what "net" funds the client ends up with reflects a higher amount by using the lawyer.

In serious cases, there is no question that an attorney is vital. The value of a serious case is often impossible to predict with accuracy, because there are so many variable factors involved. Many of these I mentioned above. Let's take a look at just two of these factors and why lawyers don't want to address the value issue at the beginning of the case.

First, jurisdiction (the location of where your case would be heard if a settlement cannot be reached) can be a very significant value predictor. In Maryland, Prince George's County and Baltimore City have reputations as being very "plaintiff friendly", compared to Montgomery County and Baltimore County. So the same case usually gets more money in the plaintiff friendly courts. Lawyers often purposely file their lawsuits in "better" jurisdictions where they have choices, because the results can be very different. In Virginia, Arlington County is considered a good "Northern Virginia" jurisdiction and Fairfax County is considered a very conservative jurisdiction. Having said all of that, good cases generally should produce good results, so jurisdiction will not matter. Your lawyer generally won't discuss jurisdiction related value concerns with you at the beginning. At the beginning, your lawyer doesn't fully know (he or she couldn't possibly know) all of the facts which might attach to your case, some which might render jurisdiction concerns irrelevant.

Second, you are a very significant component in the value of your case. If you present well, if you speak well, if you are sincere, if you are believable, you have a better chance that a jury will award you more money than if you do not have some or all of those things going for you. This is not fair. Clearly. But these factors apply in courtrooms, the same way they present in life in general. Your lawyer is not going to tell you these things at the beginning of the case. He or she doesn't know you well enough to start this type of discussion, but he or she knows these things might ultimately affect the outcome of your case.

To conclude, as we can agree, money is the ultimate goal. That is why you hire a lawyer. But most people are uncomfortable talking about money. It's not polite. Okay, so let's be impolite. We need to talk about money. The purpose of our civil legal system is to compensate victims. Thus, a discussion about money should take place. It must take place. Good lawyers will address this issue honestly and they will also explain their reluctance to provide the "value" early on.

Do you want the truth? Your case has value, but there is no guarantee about getting that value, and no universal agreement about what that value is. I will provide a written opinion to you before we begin. Can't ask for more...
Call me: 703-761-4343 or 301-949-1515

Critical Thing #4 You May Not Be Told:
There May Not Be Enough Money

Your lawyer may not tell you that there may not be enough money to properly compensate you. He or she may omit this discussion when first hired for several good reasons, but one reason may be that they don't want to lose you as a client. If they tell you that there may not be enough money right away, you might look for another lawyer.

The amount of available money on any given auto accident case starts with an examination of the auto insurance policies. The first policy to look at is the policy covering the car that was being driven by the at fault person.

Insurance companies sell policies that have "liability" coverage to protect the people who buy those policies, in case they cause an accident. Liability in this sense means that the driver was "liable" or responsible for the accident, and the purpose of the insurance is to provide funds to the victim in the event the victim's car is damaged, or the victim suffered injuries. The insurance companies put limits on the amount of money they will pay in those situations however. The insurers have "minimum" limits that they are required to provide, and they will increase those limits when their insured pays more in premiums.

In Maryland, the insurers are required to provide limits of $30,000.00 per person, and $60,000.00 per accident. This means that in the event you cause an accident, and you have these limits, the most your insurance company has to pay to any one person who was hurt in that accident is $30,000.00. It means further that the most your insurance company has to pay to all of the injured people, in total, is $60,000.00. So, if you hit a car that has 5 people in it, and they all have very serious injuries, those 5 people can claim and potentially recover no more than $60,000.00 from your insurance company, and the most any one person of those five can get is $30,000.00.

This is a tough concept to explain to people with serious injuries and huge medical bills needing to be paid. It is like a bowl of candy and kids wanting the candy. There are 10 kids, but only three pieces of candy. You've now got seven very unhappy, screaming, ranting, raving, jumping up and down kids.

No matter what the injuries are, even death, no matter what the medical bills are, even $200,000.00, no matter how long the victim missed work, no matter what permanent disability there is (can never walk again), in Maryland, if there is a minimum limits policy of $30,000.00, the victim can only recover $30,000.00.

In Virginia it is a bit worse. The minimum limits are $25,000.00 per person and $50,000.00 per accident.

Insurance companies are horrible animals. Their agents sell these minimum limits policies to people and tell them they have "full coverage," leaving them with the impression that they have good insurance protection. The reason the insurance companies sell these pitiful policies is because they want to make the sale, and the premium for a minimum limits policy is less than the premium for a bigger, better policy. In addition, the risk to the insurance company is smaller. So, the insurance company would rather sell 10 small policies and collect 10 small premiums, and have only the minimum limits as their exposure if an accident happens and is caused by those people. If they sell bigger, better policies, their financial exposure goes up, and it is not made up for by the larger premiums.

The individual who buys a minimum limits automobile insurance policy is at severe financial risk.

A "good" policy will have limits of $100,000.00 or more per person, and $300,000.00 or more per accident. I am a cautious person. I have an auto policy with limits of one million dollars.

The additional cost to get the better policy is not much more than the cost of the minimum limits policy. That is why the insurance companies do not want to sell it to you, and that is why their agents usually don't tell you about it unless you ask.

Let's go back to the sources of money for you if you have been injured. Again, the first is the other guy's insurance. Next, there is the auto insurance covering the car you were in at the time of the accident.

The coverage we want to look at for the car you were in is called Uninsured Motorist coverage, which includes Under-insured Motorist coverage. Your attorney will absolutely ask you about your insurance, and he or she will ask you to provide a copy of your insurance policy so they can see what amount of coverage you have.

Uninsured and Under-Insured coverage works like this: you can make a claim against your insurance company for the difference "above" the limit of the at fault person's insurance if your injuries warrant compensation that is more than the other person's limits. Here is an example:

Suppose you have a severe injury and you end up with $75,000.00 in medical bills. Suppose we agree that your case has a value well over $100,000.00, because the bills are $75,000.00 and your suffering is worth more than $25,0000.00. Suppose that the other person, who caused the accident, has a Maryland minimum limits auto insurance policy. This means that you can only get $30,000.00 from that person's insurance.

Suppose further that you have a policy that has Uninsured Motorist coverage of $100,000.00 per person. Usually, by the way, the Uninsured Motorist coverage is the same as the Liability coverage. I told you that Uninsured Motorist coverage includes what is called Under-Insured Motorist coverage. In the example I'm providing here, the other guy doesn't' have enough insurance coverage to fully compensate you. So in this situation he is "under-insured." You can use your insurance policy to make up the shortage, and you could claim and potentially recover up to $80,000.00 from your insurance company. You can only claim and recover $70,000.00 because your insurance company gets a "credit" for the $30,000.00 that the other guy's insurance paid, so you can get your full "policy limits" ($100,000.00) minus the other guy's limits ($30,000.00), which equals $70,000.00 from your company.

Now imagine that your insurance limit is $30,000.00. You would get ZERO from them in the above case.

Would you be upset because there was not enough? Now you can only blame yourself (and again maybe your insurance agent if they didn't explain all of this), because you bought the policy with those limits. If you had higher limits, potentially you could get more.

In the event the other person had no insurance coverage, at all, then you can use your insurance under the Uninsured Motorist coverage to claim and potentially recover funds all the way up to your limit.

I said that a $100,000.00 per person $300,000.00 per accident policy is a good policy. In most cases it is. Your tolerance for payment and risk protection should govern what you do, but at least now you know the considerations.

So, reviewing, first is the other guy's auto policy, second is the policy of the car you were in at the time of the accident. Now we stop and ask: Was the car you were in at the time of the accident your car? If yes, the next source of insurance coverage we can look for is coverage that might be available from other cars owned by relatives who live in your household. If your brother, or mom lives in your house, and they own a car that is insured on an auto policy that is different than your policy (it can be the same insurance company, but just a different policy), you can recover additional funds from that policy up to the full limit of that policy.

So again, let's continue with the prior example. Suppose you've recovered $30,000.00 from the other guy's insurance, and you recovered $70,000.00 from your company. Let's suppose your brother lives in your house and he owns a car and he has insurance of $50,000.00. You can now claim and potentially recover that full $50,000.00 from his policy. Let's further suppose your sister lives in your house and she also owns a car and has it insured for $50,000.00. You can also claim and potentially recover up to $50,000.00 from her policy. In the language of insurance, this process is called "stacking."

I asked above if the car you were in at the time of the accident was your car. I answered "yes" and provided discussion. Now let's answer 'no". Let's say the car you were in at the time of the accident belonged to your friend. The next auto policy you can go after in this case, after your friend's policy, is your own auto policy. Thereafter, you can pursue the policies of your relatives who own cars and who live in the same house as you.

Follow all of this? Make sure your attorney fully explains all of it to your complete satisfaction.

Note: if you are my client, you will get this explanation!

Okay, finding money doesn't end here. The other guy may have "umbrella" coverage. That is a policy that protects against mostly all things that result in him owing money. A good injury attorney will check this out for you in the appropriate case.

Another source of money is the cash and assets of the other guy. Also, there are his wages. In truth, pursuing the other guy "personally" (meaning beyond insurance) usually doesn't result in obtaining anything. There are many and sometimes complicated reasons for this, but the easiest reasons to understand might be first, the guy simply doesn't' have any assets, second that the guy can declare bankruptcy and then your legal entitlement evaporates, and finally, he can change jobs and you'd be in a perpetual search process, following him around, or paying someone to follow him, to learn where he's working and trying to take what the laws allow you take (it's never his full salary).

Your lawyer probably won't tell you about pursuing the other guy personally at first, because he doesn't know if the case will ever get that far or need to have that information. If and when the time comes for this information, the lawyer will run an "asset check" on the other guy.

To conclude, your lawyer probably won't tell you up front that there might not be enough money to fully compensate you. It would be very upsetting to hear.

What does a good lawyer do if there is not enough money to fully compensate his client? Many will seek discounts on the medical bills to at least try to make sure the client doesn't owe any money.

I have handled too many cases where clients' injuries were severe and the medical bills were staggering. I can proudly say that I have never had a case, where at the end, my clients owed any money to anyone. I have always been able to get discounts to assure "no debt." I have been fortunate and skilled enough to accomplish that in every case I've ever had where the situation presented.

Make sure you ask your attorney about this situation if it applies to you.

Getting better insurance may be the most important lesson
I can teach you.

I will provide you with an absolutely FREE review of your
Insurance Policy. You can even send it to me by FAX or email and I
will reply. Most people do not want to take the time for something
like this. Therefore, I will make it easy for you. My fax # is 703-761-
4349. My email is paul@samakowlaw.com. All I need is your
"Declarations Page" to see what you have and what you do not.

Critical Thing #5 You May Not Be Told:
Justice is Rare.

You hire an attorney to help with negative things that happened to you because of a car accident; sometimes horrible, certainly always inconvenient, and often there are things you can't or don't want to try to resolve yourself. Consequences include getting your car fixed, dealing with the insurance companies, figuring out how to get medical help, how to pay for medical bills, and getting reimbursed for time lost from your job. It is rare that a client goes to a lawyer after a car accident and wants "justice". Money is the predominant need and goal. But sometimes, later, as immediate goals get resolved, clients develop ideas about getting "justice."

Over the years I've had many clients who were victims of drunk drivers. We understand that accidents can happen. Feelings and emotions are different however when the accident was caused by a drunk driver. Society wants drunk drivers punished, locked up and some want more. There is a need for "justice."

Unfortunately, your auto accident lawyer won't tell you that you can't get justice. By the way, what is justice? Our civil legal system in these cases provides only monetary compensation and requires those who were at fault (or their insurance companies) to pay the victims. What makes it hard to understand is that many people don't understand the difference between the "civil" and "criminal" processes of our legal system.

Civil "justice" is premised upon the "you broke it, you pay for it" concept. Money is the only available answer in car accident cases.

Criminal laws are there to punish the bad guys who intended to do bad stuff. Someone who was speeding or simply who wasn't paying attention, and who truly had no intent to do anything bad, isn't going to be criminally prosecuted by the authorities. They might get a traffic court citation and have to pay a fine, and in some cases if the individual's driving behavior was aggravated, or was a repeated offense, jail-time is possible.

The point is, your lawyer isn't the prosecutor, and he or she can't do anything to obtain any form of criminal punishment for the other driver. What your lawyer hopefully can and will do is get you money to compensate for your losses and damages.

So I'm back to justice. Would you voluntarily suffer all of the aggravation of a car accident, including having to then get your car repaired, having a sore neck and back, and having to go to get medical care for a month or two, and miss time from work, for say, $10,000.00? How about for $15,000.00? What is your price? What amount of money makes those things okay? Okay, let's not be ridiculous. You're not going to get a million dollars for a fender bender. And if you suffered permanent, disabling injuries, a million dollars isn't enough and no amount would be enough. As the saying goes "without your health, there's nothing." Is there any justice to be obtained here? You get my point, I'm sure. There is no amount of money that you would readily exchange to be hurt, to miss work, etc.

Your auto accident attorney isn't going to tell you that you can't get justice. Instead, you'll hear that you will be fairly compensated for your losses, damages, injuries, etc. Your attorney will tell you that he or she will get you the most money there is to be gotten in a case like yours. But you won't hear that the money is "just" or "fair."

Critical Thing #6 You May Not Be Told:
Justice is an Illusion

Now that you have learned that justice is rare I want to continue to educate you and inform you that your attorney won't tell you that justice is an illusion. I want to redefine justice here. I want to now use the word to mean that the end result of your car accident case is acceptable to you. This continues the discussion from the prior section where I discussed that there really is no amount of money that can be given to you at the end of your case that makes everything "worth it" or "okay."

Your attorney will not tell you that the money you get at the end will make things that happened "okay." He or she will not tell you that the money you receive will somehow be worth your bad experiences.

Your attorney will not tell you that at the end, in most cases, you will get an amount of money that is insulting. Your attorney will not tell you up front that if your case cannot "settle" for a fair amount of money that going to court is normally not an option, or that going to court could result in you obtaining even less money than the settlement would produce. The truth is, most small and even moderate car accident injury cases that go to court do not result in exceptionally better results than settlements. Your attorney will not initially tell you that going to court is not really a good choice in most cases and that you could actually win your case and end up with no money.

So as you're reading this, you're thinking "Why do I need an attorney?" Keep reading.

Going to court can produce excellent results. The problem is, often, in small and moderate cases, court fees and an increased attorney's fee will leave you with less money than the original settlement offer. Next, even if you get a bit more money in court, it might not be "worth it" when you consider (1) the delay in getting to court (anywhere from 5 months to 2 years, depending upon the jurisdiction and whether you filed your lawsuit in the smaller District Court, or the more formal and larger Circuit Court), and (2) the time off of work you'll have to spend assisting in the litigation process.

Finally, you should understand that going to court is always a risk, and that the amount of the verdict isn't guaranteed. Thus, you could actually end up, after a bad verdict, with less money than the insurance company was willing to give you, with no money, or even owing money! So going to court isn't always a great idea. One last thought. If you go to court, you could actually lose the case! Yes, even though the accident wasn't your fault, you could lose. Strange things happen in courtrooms.

This truth, that going to court is not always a great idea, comes to you as a result of the terrific brain washing of the public (who comprise our juries) that the insurance industry orchestrated over the last 15 years.... but that's another story and a topic for another book.... But I'll discuss it a little bit. Have you ever heard about frivolous lawsuits? Tort reform? People who whine and complain about little accidents? People who try to take advantage of the insurance companies? Have you heard the expression "greedy trial lawyers?" All of these phrases come to you via the insurance industry, who invented them to convince the public that people who get into car accidents (and people injured in other ways) don't deserve the money that they, the insurance industry ultimately will have to pay. Hear about the "McDonald's lady" who got coffee spilled on her? I'll bet you believe that the amount of money she got was absurd. That's because you heard wrong. The truth is that she didn't get the millions that were reported, yet that case became the rallying cry of the insurers and others who don't feel that responsible parties should pay for the troubles they create. Go to your computer and Google the name Stella Liebeck and read the truth about what happened to that nice lady who had third degree burns on her inner thighs from 180 degree coffee, and how all she wanted was for McDonalds to pay for her medical bills.

Back to the "no justice" concept. Justice is available (if money can equal justice), just not usually, and rarely for small cases.

So why is your attorney hiding this information? Because if he or she tells you that justice is an illusion, you won't hire him or her. You will likely go to another attorney and ask if you can "get justice" or if going to court can be your back-up plan, and that attorney will either tell you the truth, or lie to you to get the case.

Your lawyer will tell you his or her value to you. You will be outraged when you learn that without an attorney, you'll get even less money, in fact, you'll get so little from the insurance company if you try to do this yourself that you'd probably want to reach through the telephone and strangle the adjuster. Having the attorney on you side levels the playing field, keeps the insurance companies on guard, and usually guarantees you'll get the most money that there is to be recovered.

Adjust your thinking if you've been in an accident. You need a lawyer most of time and you'll get more money using a lawyer, even after the lawyer's fee is taken out. Remember I told you about a group called the Insurance Institute? They publish statistics every year, about seemingly a trillion things. One of the findings each year reveals that people with attorneys, on average, get about three times more than people without attorneys. So, being in an accident isn't about getting justice. Our legal system doesn't have a better answer than giving you money to attempt to compensate you for what happened.

30

Critical Thing #7 You May Not Be Told:
Lawyers are Pessimists

Your auto accident lawyer will not tell you his or her true nature. The longer he or she has been a lawyer, the more skill they have accumulated over the years, and the more pessimistic they become. That is because practicing law is an exercise in predicting what can go wrong and planning and strategizing how to avoid all of the bad outcomes.

"It appears you have a good case, and we should be able to do well for you and get you good results." This is more likely what your lawyer will tell you at the beginning. Your lawyer doesn't know all of the facts at the beginning. He doesn't know who all of the witnesses are, and how convincing they may be.... He doesn't know if the witnesses will change their stories later on. He doesn't know everything about you.

Lawyers will act like guarded optimists. "Yes! You have a great case!" These words are rarely heard from good lawyers. Why not? Because good lawyers know there is much that can wrong, and that cases can turn on facts, the law, impressions, choice of words, and much more.

Allow me to share an example of how things can go wrong, that hopefully illustrates why good lawyers are guarded and rarely promise results.

I had a case a few years ago where a young lady was seriously injured in a one- car accident. She was a back seat passenger. She was with her boyfriend's friend, and another young man, who picked her up to go to a party. The police report reflected that the driver lost control and the car ended up hitting an embankment and rolling down into a ditch. My client needed surgery on her back and left leg. They had to put a rod into her leg to help the bones grow back properly and calcify.

My client's mother was a previous client. The mother called me from the hospital on the night of the accident. I went to the hospital the next day and the young lady told me the story. She told me the driver dozed briefly, lost control, and then the accident happened. I was told the other passenger already had a lawyer. I asked my young client and her mother to get me the name of the other lawyer, so we could coordinate our strategy.

Despite my continued requests, I never got the information about the other lawyer, and my client told me that the other passenger would not talk to me. The driver's insurance company did not know if the other passenger had a lawyer. (One of the first things we auto accident lawyers do is send a letter to the insurance companies telling them that we represent the client, so that way they insurance adjusters don't call the clients and bother them or try to get them to say potentially hazardous things). I felt something was wrong with this whole matter, but I pressed on, because my client had serious and permanent injuries deserving of compensation, and because her story about what happened and the police report were consistent. Over the many months that passed, I probably had five or six long conversations with my client going over all of the facts of the accident. She was always consistent. Finally, the police never charged the driver with any traffic court charge because, perhaps, they felt he didn't need extra aggravation. The driver too had serious injuries.

The insurance company for the driver would not agree to offer any settlement of the case, at all. I was puzzled. I couldn't figure out why not. I asked if they had facts or information I didn't have. I was told that my client had something to do with causing the accident. The insurance adjuster wouldn't tell me more than that. I immediately asked my client. She swore on the proverbial "stack of bibles" that she had no idea what the adjuster was talking about. So I filed a lawsuit. Part of the lawsuit process is discovering evidence about the other side's case. That means I finally might get to talk to the driver and to the other passenger. These "talks" are called depositions. The lawyers ask questions, and the deponents have to answer, under a sworn oath that they'll tell the truth, just as it would be in court. The defense lawyer and I agreed to do the depositions on the same day. At this point nobody knew where the other passenger was, at least according to my client. She told me he moved to Tennessee, she "heard". I pressed her on this and she told me not to worry, because he was on her side against the driver, so even if the driver's attorney found him, he would help us....

We started the depositions by the defense attorney asking my client questions. During this painful, agonizing hour, I learned, for the first time, that my client, age 17, had a child when she was 14, that she had had been suspended at school twice in the last year for fighting, and that she had a Facebook page that was critical of blacks. As these fun things to tell at Show & Tell came out, one by one, I wondered if somehow I didn't do my job preparing. Clearly, I know clients lie. But all of this? My client's character was now registering somewhere just above drug dealers. Oh! My client's sister was a drug dealer (as I'd soon learn). How could I have known she had a child? There was no way I could check school records, and I had heard of Facebook, but didn't know what it was much, other than it was a way for kids to talk to each other on-line.

The revelations of this day were startling. Before, everything was consistent. I even had a good opinion of my client by association, because my client's mother, a former client, was a fine and honorable woman. My client's "case" just dropped in value significantly, because even if I could keep the jury from hearing some of those things, likely I wouldn't be successful in keeping all of it out. None of those things were relevant to how the accident happened, nor to my client's injuries, but what I didn't know yet was that the fighting at school thing was going to tie into the driver's story.

By the defense lawyer's questions, I soon got bits and pieces of what the driver was going to say. I learned about my client's sister. My client admitted her sister was in jail for selling drugs. I learned that the driver was going to say that my client grabbed the steering wheel. My client, when that came out, shook her head vehemently motioning denial. After her deposition I took my young client out of the room and asked her, point blank, yes or no, if she grabbed the steering wheel of the car. She continued to deny that she was anywhere near the steering wheel. At this point, some of you reading this, perhaps knowledgeable a bit about deposition strategy, might ask how all of these things came out, if they're not relevant. Lawyers don't usually object to too many questions at depositions, because at depositions, the test for asking questions is not if the question or answer is relevant, but only if the answer might lead to some information that could be relevant. So many lawyers will allow the other lawyer to ask just about anything, except for things about say for example sexual preferences. And even that information could lead to the discovery of some relevant information.

So then I proceeded with my deposition, asking the driver questions. He was a pleasant looking, very well spoken college student who was dressed immaculately. He was the type of young man, by appearance and first impression anyway, that would impress anyone. His story was that during the car ride to the party, he made a comment to my client about her sister, who as we now knew was currently serving a prison sentence for selling drugs. Before that day, by the way, I was never told about the existence of a sister, much less her criminal conviction or her current residence. The young man volunteered that the comment he made was not a nice thing to say (I won't repeat it here because this is a PG book) and that he was trying to tease my client. He said that upon hearing the remark about her sister, my client leaned forward from the back seat, hit him in the chest, and then grabbed the steering wheel, both of which he said happened almost simultaneously, and that he lost control of the steering wheel and the accident happened. You can imagine my otherwise everyday calm demeanor turning livid, realizing that my client had lied to me. This young man was thoroughly, completely believable.

I heard his story, and then took my client to another room and asked her again about what he had said and about her grabbing the steering wheel. She admitted all of it was true.

I went back into the room and told the defense lawyer that I might be withdrawing from the case because of strategic differences with my client. Ethically, I could not now let my client go to court and lie, and I could not allow her to tell the truth, because first, we'd lose, as she contributed to the accident, and second, even if somehow the jury believed it wasn't her fault and that it was reasonable for her to hit a driver of a car in motion and grab the steering wheel, well, the whole story about her wonderful personality would come out, because it was now very relevant, and the jury would despise her and not award her any damages. I dropped the case, told my client good luck, and considered myself lucky that I learned all of this before trial, so that I would not be professionally embarrassed in front of a judge and in a public forum.

All good lawyers know lots of disaster stories. All good lawyers know that cases can explode, or implode. Lawyers are therefore pessimists. They spare no expense, they leave no rock unturned, they stop at nothing, they stay up at night, they talk to themselves in the mirror, they do anything and everything to figure out the problems. Good lawyers do this so they can avoid problems or minimize them, to ultimately produce a good result. Good lawyers worry about every detail imaginable, and details other normal people would never even think of, or if they did, wouldn't worry about. Good lawyers look at things from the glass is one-tenth full view. Good lawyers worry so you don't have to. Good lawyers need to get a *Life is Good* T-Shirt.

Good lawyers are pessimists. Good lawyers are good because they are pessimists.

Because they are good lawyers, they will not tell you about their inner pessimistic personality. Who wants a pessimist fighting for them? You do. Let's figure out EVERYTHING that can go wrong, and then we can get you the best possible result.

Good lawyers will act optimistically, to a point, because that's good business. You wouldn't hire a lawyer if he told you "you're no good, your case is no good, and you may not get a good result, but hire me and I'll try real hard."

If you get a good result, buy your lawyer the T-Shirt and say thanks.

Critical Thing #8 You May Not Be Told:
You Can Fire Me

Well, what an interesting concept. Likely your attorney isn't going to tell you this. He or she has spent way too much time, effort, and money to get you in the door to become a client. Why would any businessperson invite you in and then announce that you can leave? Attorneys, like other business people, want you to stay. The mere thought of mentioning this concept to a client clearly sends ripples through most attorneys.

"Your can fire me" isn't a ripple for an auto accident attorney; it's a tsunami wave. Compare an accident lawyer getting fired and another, hourly fee basis lawyer who gets fired. For the average lawyer working on an hourly fee basis, if you fire him, you will owe him for the time he has spent on your case. The hourly fee has probably already been partially paid by the client in the form of a retainer. Goodness, divorce lawyers take thousands of dollars up front and charge their hourly work for you against the retainer you gave them when you hired them. Before your retainer hits zero, you get an itemized statement showing you the hours spent and a love note to please send another $X dollars to restock the retainer pot.

With auto accident attorneys, there is no retainer for the work, because the fee is contingent, that is, it is based on outcome, usually a percentage equivalent to one-third of the recovery against the at-fault person's insurance company. The law governs when the accident lawyer's fee is "earned", and that is, basically, when the job is completed. So, if you fire your lawyer somewhere in the process, before the case is over, the lawyer can't send you a bill.

All states have laws that somewhat protect the attorney who has been fired by her client. The laws allow the attorney to recover their costs, that is, any expenses they advanced for the client, and a reasonable amount for their professional services up to the point of being fired, calculated by their normal hourly fee, multiplied by the number of hours they worked on your case.

That lawyer protection device is called "putting a lien" on the case. Lawyers are not going to tell you that you can fire them, so it follows that they also are not going to tell you that if you do fire them, the will put a lien on your case.

In fairness, there are some attorneys and law firms that do disclose these things to their clients at the very first meeting, and they even put this discussion in the contract, sometimes called a "Fee Agreement" or an "Attorney-Client Agreement." But most attorneys will not ever discuss these concepts with you. The thinking is that you are in their office, however it is you got there, and now they have an opportunity to take on your case, to impress you so later you'll refer your friends, and to make money. Why put the thought in your head that you can fire them?

Among all of the things that auto accident lawyers normally don't or won't tell you, this one is probably the least offensive. But you should know. You can fire your attorney. If she puts a lien on your case, that's okay. She deserves to be paid for what she's done thus far, and certainly she's entitled to get back any money she advanced for you. What follows is that then, you're probably going to get another attorney. Make sure that the new attorney doesn't charge you the full fee. The new attorney should accept your case and agree that she will take the other lawyer's fee out of her fee. That way, you are not being charged a one-third fee plus the first lawyer's fee.

Not everyone clicks with everyone else. I have been on both sides of the fence during my career as an attorney. For various reasons, I've had clients fire me (fortunately, not too many), and I've also had clients come to me telling me they fired their first attorney. It isn't right that the client should be penalized for having the attorney of their choice. If lawyer #1, for whatever reason, isn't the right one, the client should not be suffering and feeling that they're stuck because they'll have to pay extra to get another attorney. They should know they can fire their attorney and that they won't have to pay extra to get lawyer #2.

Give your attorney the benefit of the doubt about how your case is going. Don't jump to fire her until you give her the opportunity to address your issues and concerns. The number one problem of all clients, across all practice areas of law (including auto accident lawyers), and in every state, and the number one complaint of clients to Bar Associations, is that the lawyer doesn't communicate with them (or not enough). Tell your accident lawyer you want regular communication and regular updates. Be proactive and call if you're not getting the information you need or want. If the relationship goes so sour you can no longer handle it, then, after one more chance to rectify things, it is legal, and it is okay, to fire your lawyer.

Chapter 3

The Right Attorney for Your Automobile Accident Case

Now that I have told you everything that I can think of that your auto accident attorney probably won't tell you, I will provide you with a description of what I believe that attorney should be doing for you.

Again, all of this is based on my experience as an attorney after years of handling all measure of injury matters. Other attorneys, other excellent attorneys may do things somewhat differently, and that does not mean their methods are not proper. I want you to have some basic understandings of what, in my opinion, an attorney should do and how an attorney should act when handling the routine auto accident case. These standards certainly apply to cases involving more serious injuries. However, I have written this with the routine case in mind, as that imaginary routine case is the one that occurs most often. I believe that there are absolute "rights" and "wrongs" in the handling of an auto claim.

An Accident Happens.

You have just been involved in an automobile accident that was not your fault. Your car is all banged up; you are hurt; you are probably worried about many of the consequences this accident has now created, and "this just wasn't a good time for this kind of thing". There are 101 things racing through your mind. Certainly, the last thing you need to worry about is finding a good attorney to handle matters for you. Hopefully this information, together with the knowledge you've now gained by reading this book to this point, will give you a leg up on making that search a bit easier, by allowing you to know what to look for, and by allowing you to know what questions to ask. If you have a case in Virginia or Maryland, of course, I would be interested in speaking to you and I would be happy to answer your questions. If your accident happens in another jurisdiction, keep reading, and hopefully this book will prove helpful to you.

Find an Attorney to Help!

Finding an attorney is easy. Finding the right attorney might be a little tougher. First, understand that there is nothing immediately critical about hiring an attorney. I recommend, however, that you do so within 2 - 3 days of the accident. In this fashion you can avoid being hassled by insurance adjusters, and an intelligent course of action for you and your case can be formulated. Back to finding that attorney... If you have a good case, there are hundreds of attorneys who will be thrilled to work for you. Legal fees for "personal injury" cases can be very handsome. Such fees for the right attorney however, are well worth it. Read on, and you'll see why.

You should be able to recognize a sincere appreciative attitude on the part of the attorney you select. Again, there are hundreds of attorneys who'd be very happy to have you as a client. If the attorney you select isn't one of them, find one who is. That attorney will work very hard for you. Keep reading and I'll help you learn how to pick the right attorney.

First Stages and First Contact.

Your car is in need of repair, you are in need of medical treatment, and your ability to go to work at this point is in doubt, both because you now lack transportation, and because you don't feel physically able to do so. Insurance adjusters are calling. What should you do? A good attorney can tell you. A good attorney will also find out many important things, such as: did the police investigate? Was the other party given a ticket? Who is the other guy? Is there insurance? Is there enough insurance? Again, a good attorney will advise you about what to do, and find out the answers to all of these questions. You need to concentrate on getting better. Investigating these matters and spending hours on the telephone are the last things on the doctor's prescription pad for you.

Good attorneys can be found in many places. Start with your friends and family. Ask them if they have ever been injured and if they hired a lawyer. Ask them how they liked that lawyer. Ask your doctor if he regularly treats injury victims and if he can recommend a lawyer. Go to the local bar association referral service. If there isn't such a thing, or if they're not open and you want contact now, go to an internet search engine (Google, Yahoo, Bing, MSN, E-LocalLawyers) and type in the name of your city and state, followed by "auto accident lawyer" or "injury lawyer". Look at several websites critically and use the information here to analyze the lawyer. Wherever you find the lawyer, don't jump without asking a lot of questions.

The First Telephone Call.

You select an attorney and you want to call him or her. Pay attention to several things: Is the number you are calling advertised as 24 hours? If so, who answers the call? Is it a tape? Is it the staff? Is it the attorney? Any may be acceptable, but clearly, you should be looking to talk to the attorney within a reasonable time if that first call doesn't get you connected to him or her. Next, should you call "off-hours", or wait until business hours Monday through Friday, 9 - 5? My feeling is that an attorney who practices injury law must recognize that potential clients are calling, often very traumatized, often very confused, and often in need of some good solid advice. Accordingly, that attorney should be available whenever the potential client calls. So you call, and you are generally pleased. The attorney sounded okay, and invites you to his or her office for an appointment. Before you go in, ask some questions:

1. How long has the attorney been in practice? You want someone with experience.
2. What percentage of the attorney's caseload involves handling personal injury matters? It should be over 80%.
3. Does the attorney regularly go to court and fight for his clients when it involves injury matters? Yes is the only acceptable answer.
4. Is the attorney accessible? Get a commitment that you'll be able to speak to the attorney, if you want to, within a reasonable time, every time you want to. Promise to respect the attorney's off-hours privacy, but ask if the attorney will give you a cell or mobile telephone number for emergencies.
5. Will you be kept informed of all significant developments? This means that you'll routinely get copies of important correspondence, and that you will be consulted before decisions beyond the mere routine occur.

6. How is money handled? Don't be shy about asking about this!! This is the primary reason you are hiring an attorney. Think about it... The mechanic is going to fix your car. The doctor will get you back to good health... You'll certainly ask them questions... The attorney is the person who will help get you the money from the other guy's insurance company to pay for all of this!

The First Meeting.

You're satisfied with the telephone contact and you agree to meet with the attorney you've called. At this meeting you should meet the attorney, talk with him or her for as long as you want, and the entire process should be explained to you. This includes all of the things I've discussed in this book, and specifically explaining all of the possible insurance benefits available to you from all sources, including your own insurance company, and how and when such benefits are to be expected. It also means explaining, at least in summary fashion, the laws that govern your case. Different states have different laws that control "liability" issues and ultimately affect compensation. Ask your attorney to explain contributory negligence principles to you. This means that if you contributed to the accident you are not going to be able to make a claim against the other person, even if that other person was 99% at fault. A pretty harsh law, but it is the law in Maryland and Virginia.

At this first meeting, which is really the beginning of your case, your attorney CANNOT predict how much money you're going to get for your injuries. Nobody knows, at the early stages, how badly you are hurt, how much medical care you're going to need, how much time you might miss from work, or even the potential legal theories which might be available. Can you predict the final score of a baseball game in the first inning? IT IS RIDICULOUS FOR AN ATTORNEY TO ATTEMPT TO ESTIMATE HOW MUCH YOU'RE GOING TO GET AT THE BEGINNING OF THE CASE.

At the initial meeting a paralegal or other staff member may take "administrative" information from you. The attorney should explain the legal contract, or fee agreement, with you. Attorney's fees in this type of case are almost universally "contingent fees", which means the attorney only gets paid when the case is settled;

that is, the fee is "contingent" upon resolution. Usually attorneys charge one-third of the recovery, and usually contracts of this sort detail a higher fee, perhaps 40 - 50%, if the case goes to trial. This is fair; because going to trial is a lot more work for the attorney, and involves the attorney taking on a lot more risk. Recognize that every "contingent fee" case an attorney takes on is a case where the attorney is working for free, and at great risk of getting nothing, until (and unless) the case resolves.

How the First Meeting Should End.

Your initial meeting with your attorney should conclude with you receiving a copy of the fee agreement, and with a very concrete list of things that should be set to happen.

1. You should have a list of things the attorney needs, such as a copy of your insurance policy, pay stubs, tax returns, photographs, etc.

2. Telephone calls should be made promptly for the resolution of the damage to your car. The two most typical scenarios are as follows:
    a) The car is repairable. If it's in a tow-lot, plans should be set to get it out, as storage charges accrue quickly. Next, insurers should be notified of the location of the car, so an appraisal of damage can take place. If the insurers can be notified quickly, often they will move it out of the towing lot. In any event, discussion as to what's going to happen one way or the other should be presented to you.
    b) The car is destroyed, or "totaled". If there is an outstanding loan on the car, you must supply the lender's name and account number to your attorney so they can contact them to discuss payoff. Again, insurers must be notified of the car's location, so it can be moved and they can appraise the value. You will have to sign over the title to the car, so be prepared to make it available quickly. If there's a loan, usually the lender has the title, or a part of the title.

3. Plans should be set for you to get alternate transportation. Any good personal injury attorney should be able to recommend a reputable rental car company.

4. Plans should be set for you to get "the right type" of medical care. This means, in most cases, that you should be treating with an orthopedic physician, a chiropractor, or a general practice physician who provides physical therapy services. If you don't have a family doctor who can refer you to "the right type" of doctor, or if you don't know someone who knows such a doctor, your attorney should be able to give you the names of several reputable physicians near where you live or work. It is essential that you receive medical care if you are hurt, and that you get this care as soon as possible. Medical study after medical study shows that individuals who start medical treatment later end up needing more medical treatment than they would have if they had begun that treatment soon after the trauma occurred.

   a) Good injury attorneys have many medical "contacts". If needed, arrangements often can be made through your attorney allowing you to receive medical care without payment up front (or as you go). This is accomplished by a document called an "Assignment". Both you and your attorney sign this document, and thereby agree that the doctor will get paid at the end of your case, from the proceeds recovered. In this fashion, the doctor is satisfied, because of the attorney's reputation, that payment will probably be forthcoming. Your attorney should tell you that the signing of this document does not eliminate your responsibility for payment.

5. Your attorney's office should send out several letters within the first 24 hours after meeting with you. At a minimum, these letters go to:

   a) insurance companies advising that you are now represented, and advising that all contact about your case should go through the attorney's office;

   b) medical care facilities, requesting records, reports and bills;

c) accident witnesses, asking for statements, or requesting appointments to review what they saw or what they know;

d) investigating police, requesting the accident report.

The "Middle Stages," Where You are Physically Recovering.

Your attorney and his or her staff are now acting as both a "collection facility", gathering records and bills from medical care providers, and continuing as a shield, keeping the insurance company representatives away from you. I often have clients call me and ask me "how's my case going?" If case liability is not an issue, that is, if it's clear that the accident was "the other guy's" fault, and his/her insurance company has "accepted" responsibility, then my answer to the question is simply "fine, how are you feeling?" I say this because at that point, assuming we've "secured" the liability issue, all that remains is waiting for the client to get better.

A good injury attorney is able to review medical records and spot problems. I have called doctors and have asked them to correct mistakes in the medical records. It is actually amazing sometimes. Records sometimes misstate gender, referring to a man as "she or her" or a woman as "he or him." These little things would not seem like a big deal to the average person, but they give the defense lawyer, if the case goes to trial, the ability to pick at the doctor when he or she testifies, and to comment that maybe their medical care is sloppy, like their record-keeping. Again, remember, lawyers are pessimists and fret over EVERYTHING. I remember one medical report said "as a result of my office's therapy the patient has gotten progressively worse." Hmmmmm.... We corrected that little misstatement. I have called doctors when I have felt that certain diagnostic tests were questionable. I have called doctors when therapy seemed to be continuing endlessly without any improvement in my client's condition. I have called doctors when bills seemed out of line. Your attorney should be knowledgeable enough to do the same, and should have the gumption to do so if and when appropriate.

The Ending Stages: Evaluation of the Case and the Settlement Process.

ONCE YOU ARE COMPLETELY DONE WITH ALL MEDICAL CARE, AND ONCE YOU ARE BACK TO PRE-COLLISION STATUS, OR IF THAT'S NOT POSSIBLE, ONCE YOU'RE AS GOOD AS YOU'RE GOING TO GET, THEN, AND ONLY THEN, SHOULD YOUR ATTORNEY CONSIDER ATTEMPTING TO RESOLVE YOUR CASE.

Having said that, there are a few notable exceptions. First, the "statute of limitations" provides a limit on how long you have to either settle your case or file a lawsuit if your case cannot be settled. So, if you are not medically resolved, but the statute of limitations date is approaching, your attorney should meet with you and explain your options. The Statute of Limitations in Virginia is two years from the date the accident happened. It is three years in Maryland. Next, in many cases the total amount of insurance funds available (policy limits) may not be enough to fully compensate you. Thus, no matter how badly you have been injured, no matter how much your medical bills are, the insurance coverage available simply won't be enough. Accordingly, the question presents as to whether it is reasonable to "settle" now, given that waiting will not produce any more funds for you. It may be reasonable to attempt to resolve the case, assuming all options have been explored, if this situation presents itself. Your attorney should explain your options.

Show Me the Money.

I recognize that most people do not voluntarily position themselves to be automobile accident victims. People generally don't get hurt just so they can collect. Please don't have misgivings about seeking money here. This isn't about getting rich. This isn't about fraud or trying to take advantage of the system. When an accident occurs and you are the victim, there is absolutely nothing wrong with feeling an entitlement to money. Our civil legal system provides this, MONEY, as the only remedy. You are entitled to be compensated for medical expenses you incurred, for wages you lost, for mental and physical pain and suffering, for disfigurement, for aggravation, for inconvenience, for disrupting the quality of your life, and for more.

Any good personal injury lawyer will tell you his or her opinion concerning the value of your case, now that you have gotten to that "settlement-ready" posture. If they don't know, or don't have an opinion, what are they there for? Your attorney should set out several things in writing for you BEFORE going to the insurance company to discuss settlement. These are:

1. How much the attorney thinks your case is worth.

2. How much the attorney is going to demand. Clearly, in the upcoming process of discussion with the insurance adjuster, the attorney must have room to negotiate.

3. How much you owe in outstanding medical bills. This will affect the "net funds" you receive.

4. Whether there are liens against the proceeds of your settlement. Health insurance, worker's compensation, or a federal, state or local agency (Medicare, Medicaid) may have made some payments for your medical bills or to you for wages you lost. These groups may be entitled to be reimbursed. Again, this will affect the "net funds" you receive.

5. What options are available if settlement negotiations do not result in an acceptable resolution?

6. Is the lawyer going to attempt to mediate? arbitrate? litigate? You should know what all of these options are, if they are available, and what the pluses and minuses are with each. AND THESE should be compared to the settlement possibilities. Examples, in exact dollars, should be provided to you to allow you to see the differences. If you get a settlement offer that is 95% of what you want through settlement negotiation, it probably isn't a stellar idea to file a lawsuit, which forces delay, causes extra expense, and leaves the case unresolved.

7. Who is going to negotiate? I believe that if you hire an attorney, it is fine for the attorney to delegate non-legal, administrative matters to non-lawyer staff. On the other hand, I believe the attorney you hire should be the one who gets on the telephone and negotiates your case for you.

The Very End: Hopefully a Successful Settlement.

Once the case is settled, the attorney should receive a check from the other party's insurance company. You should see this check. It should have your name on it as a payee. It's okay if it also has the attorney's name as a payee. You should sign the check. The attorney should present to you a document similar to what I call a "Settlement Memorandum". This document should detail the "money in" (the insurance check for settlement), and the "money out", that is, all of the things which are going to be paid from that check. These will include the attorney's fee, outstanding medical bills, any liens, and a "net" for you. The check should be placed into a special bank account that the attorney MUST have, called either an "escrow" account, or a "trust" account. This is an account where client funds are held, and attorneys are held to the highest of standards for the accounting of these bank accounts by attorney licensing authorities and bar associations. Routinely funds should be deposited immediately after the check is fully endorsed, and thereafter, funds should be disbursed within 5-10 days, the delay simply to allow the funds to "clear".

After Care.

Your attorney should complete all legal matters relating to your case. This means sending payment for all outstanding medical bills and liens. This means providing you with a copy of all of the checks written for those purposes. You should also either be given copies of the important items in your file (medical records, for example), or your attorney should advise you that he or she will keep them for your future needs.

Final Thoughts.

Good luck to you. Have a great life. Please drive safely as it's not just you we're concerned about. You family wants you to drive safely because they love you and depend upon you. Wear your seatbelt. Put your kids in car safety seats. Don't even think about drinking alcohol or using drugs and then getting behind the wheel. The same with texting while driving! It is actually six times MORE DANGEROUS than driving while intoxicated. Put your telephone down when you are in the car! I hope you never get into an automobile collision. If you do, I hope you don't get hurt. Remember to keep your perspective.

Remember that you are more important than your car. Take your time with the legal matters ahead of you.

Disclaimer

Please do not consider anything in this book as legal advice. Although, certainly, I believe that I know many of the arguments that the insurance companies will offer to minimize your injury claim and I believe I have a successful overall plan with the details worked out to produce excellent results for my clients in injury cases, I am not allowed to give you legal advice in this book. This book is designed to point out certain concerns, issues and problems that exist in most injury cases, but nothing here should be considered to be universal to all cases, or to necessarily apply to your case. Unless you request that I become your attorney, and unless I accept that request, and until we both sign an agreement making you my client and me your lawyer, I do not give legal advice.

Next, after you read this book you may have questions.

703-761-4343 or 301-949-1515

Please feel free to contact me and I will be happy to discuss those questions with you and to provide "general case" type of answers. I will not tell you what I think about a settlement offer you got on your case. I will not tell you what to do. Again, I will not give you specific legal advice unless I am your lawyer.

Finally, I do not want to interfere with any relationship you may have with another lawyer. If you have hired another lawyer for your injury case, and reading this book causes you to have questions or concerns, you should contact your lawyer and ask him or her those questions. Every attorney does things a bit differently, and because I say something in this book that might be different than the way it is being handled by your attorney doesn't mean that your attorney is doing it wrong. Please contact your attorney and ask questions. It is usually much better to work out problems with your attorney than to switch during your case. I do not normally accept cases in which another lawyer has been involved, unless there is something significantly wrong that cannot be remedied by the first lawyer.

Chapter 4

Bonus to 2014 Edition—Checklist of Other Concerns

While this book covered a great deal of information that can be used in the event of an automobile collision, there is probably no book that covers everything. Actually though, there is now one book I know of that covers almost everything. I say almost because I believe I do not know everything. Obviously, I wrote that book. I finished it in 2013; it was published by Cogent Publishing NY.

You can buy it on Amazon for less than $25.00. Search on my name. I attempted to cover EVERYTHING I could possibly think of that had to do with ANYTHING having to do with an automobile collision, and it covers being involved in a collision anywhere in the United States. The book is 302 pages long, and if I do say so myself, humbly, it should be a #1 NY TIMES RESOURCE BESTSELLER. Alas, not yet.

The book is:

The Most Comprehensive Nationwide Auto Accident Resolution Book, Ever!
Who Will Pay My Auto Accident Bills?

Protect Yourself. What to Do. What Not to Do. Law & Attorneys. Insurance Company Tactics. Doctors, Auto Repair… and More

Here is the Table of Contents for the book:

SECTION 3. Attorney Help

9.   Do You Need an Attorney?

10. What Your Attorney Does For You – A Summary

11. Details, Details, Details

SECTION 4. Compensation For Your Car

12. Car Repair and Property Damage Resolution

13. Diminished Value After Repairs

14. The Nuts and Bolts of the Repair Process

SECTION 5. Compensation For Your Injuries

15. Damages Evidence

16. What is Your Case Worth?

17. When Someone Dies

18. Compensation for Lost Wages & Income

19. Resolving Your Case: Settlement, Court, Mediation, Arbitration

20. Additional Cases

21. Punitive Damages

22. Structured Settlements

SECTION 6. Cases Other than Car vs. Car

23. Lions and Tigers and Bears

  (A) Pedestrians

  (B) Passenger vs. Driver

  (C) Bus Collisions

  (D) Truck and Commercial Vehicle Collisions

  (E) Hit & Run Accidents

  (F) Drunk Drivers

  (G) Multiple Accidents in Short Period of Time

  (H) Unlicensed Drivers

  (I) Drivers Using Vehicle Without Permission

24. Claims Against Government, Government Employees

  (A) Federal Government

  (B) State Government

SECTION 7. Limiting Laws, or Why You Cannot Keep All of the Money

25. Tort Reform

26. Liens and Laws

27. No Fault Laws

28. The Collateral Source Rule

29. Balance Billing

30. Dram Shop Laws and Social Host Liability

If you want to know what anything in the above Table of Contents is about, send me an email.

paul@samakowlaw.com

This is the end. One more time: drive safely, please. Your family needs you.

How to contact me -- real simple, call me.

My headquarters office locations:

8230 Old Courthouse Road #430
Tyson's Corner, VA 22182

703-761-4343

****

2730 University Blvd. #504
Wheaton, MD 20902

301-949-1515

Satellite locations:

Virginia: Alexandria/Arlington and Manassas
Maryland: Hyattsville and Gaithersburg